# Mexican

## COOKING

## Table of Contents

# Fiesta Appetizers

## Classic Guacamole

4 tablespoons finely chopped white onion, divided
1 or 2 fresh serrano or jalapeño peppers,* seeded
    and finely chopped
1 tablespoon plus 1½ teaspoons coarsely chopped
    fresh cilantro, divided
¼ teaspoon chopped garlic
2 large ripe avocados
1 medium tomato, peeled and chopped
1 to 2 teaspoons fresh lime juice
¼ teaspoon salt
    Corn tortilla chips

*Serrano and jalapeño peppers can sting and irritate the skin. Wear rubber
gloves when handling peppers and do not touch your eyes.

[1] Combine 2 tablespoons onion, peppers, 1 tablespoon cilantro
and garlic in large mortar. Grind with pestle until almost smooth.
(Mixture can be processed in blender, if necessary, but it may
become more watery than desired.)

[2] Cut avocados lengthwise into halves; remove and discard pits.
Scoop out avocado flesh; place in bowl. Add pepper mixture. Mash
roughly, leaving avocado slightly chunky.

[3] Add tomato, lime juice, salt and remaining 2 tablespoons onion
and 1½ teaspoons cilantro to avocado mixture; mix well. Serve
immediately. Serve with tortilla chips. *Makes about 2 cups*

**Turkey Ham Quesadillas**

# Turkey Ham Quesadillas

¼ **cup picante sauce or salsa**
4 **(7-inch) regular or whole wheat flour tortillas**
½ **cup (2 ounces) shredded Monterey Jack cheese**
¼ **cup finely chopped turkey ham or ham**
¼ **cup canned diced green chiles, drained,** *or* **1 to**
2 **tablespoons chopped jalapeño pepper***
**Nonstick cooking spray**
**Additional picante sauce or salsa for dipping**
**Sour cream**

*Jalapeño peppers can sting and irritate the skin. Wear rubber gloves when handling peppers and do not touch your eyes.*

[ 1 ] Spread 1 tablespoon picante sauce on each tortilla.

[ 2 ] Sprinkle cheese, turkey ham and chiles equally over half of each tortilla. Fold uncovered half over to make quesadilla; spray tops and bottoms of quesadillas with cooking spray.

[ 3 ] Grill on uncovered grill over medium coals 1½ minutes per side or until cheese is melted and tortillas are golden brown, turning once. Quarter each quesadilla and serve with additional picante sauce and sour cream. *Makes 8 appetizer servings*

# Chili con Queso

2 **tablespoons butter**
¼ **cup finely chopped onion**
1 **clove garlic, minced**
1 **can (8 ounces) tomato sauce**
1 **can (4 ounces) diced green chiles, drained**
2 **cups (8 ounces) shredded Cheddar cheese**
2 **cups (8 ounces) shredded Monterey Jack cheese**
**with jalapeño peppers**
**Tortilla chips and crisp raw vegetable dippers**

[ 1 ] Melt butter in large saucepan over medium heat. Add onion and garlic; cook until onion is tender. Stir in tomato sauce and chiles; reduce heat to low. Simmer 3 minutes. Gradually add cheeses; stir until cheeses are melted and mixture is evenly blended.

[ 2 ] Transfer to fondue pot or chafing dish; keep warm over heat source. Serve with tortilla chips and vegetable dippers.

*Makes 3 cups (about 12 servings)*

**Bite Size Tacos**

# Bite Size Tacos

**1 pound ground beef**
**1 package (1.25 ounces) taco seasoning mix**
**2 cups *French's*® French Fried Onions**
**¼ cup chopped fresh cilantro**
**32 bite-size round tortilla chips**
**¾ cup sour cream**
**1 cup shredded Cheddar cheese**

[1] Cook beef in nonstick skillet over medium-high heat 5 minutes or until browned; drain. Stir in taco seasoning mix, *¾ cup water, 1 cup* French Fried Onions and cilantro. Simmer 5 minutes or until flavors are blended, stirring often.

[2] Preheat oven to 350°F. Arrange tortilla chips on foil-lined baking sheet. Top with beef mixture, sour cream, remaining onions and cheese.

[3] Bake 5 minutes or until cheese is melted and onions are golden.
*Makes 8 appetizer servings*

# Nachos Olé

**1½ cups (6 ounces) shredded Monterey Jack cheese**
**1½ cups (6 ounces) shredded Cheddar cheese**
**1½ cups refried beans**
**72 packaged corn tortilla chips**
**1 large tomato, seeded and chopped**
**½ cup pickled jalapeño peppers, thinly sliced**

[1] Preheat oven to 400°F. Combine cheeses in small bowl.

[2] Cook and stir beans in small saucepan over medium heat until hot. Spread 1 teaspoon beans onto each tortilla chip. Arrange chips in single layer on 2 to 3 baking sheets. Sprinkle chips evenly with tomato and jalapeños; sprinkle with cheese mixture.

[3] Bake 5 to 8 minutes or until cheese is bubbly and melted.
*Makes 6 to 8 servings*

Easy Sausage Empanadas

# Easy Sausage Empanadas

**¼ pound bulk pork sausage**
**1 (15-ounce) package refrigerated pie crusts (2 crusts)**
**2 tablespoons finely chopped onion**
**⅛ teaspoon garlic powder**
**⅛ teaspoon ground cumin**
**⅛ teaspoon dried oregano**
**1 tablespoon chopped pimiento-stuffed olives**
**1 tablespoon chopped raisins**
**1 egg, separated**

Let pie crusts stand at room temperature for 20 minutes or according to package directions. Crumble sausage into medium skillet. Add onion, garlic powder, cumin and oregano; cook over medium-high heat until sausage is no longer pink. Drain drippings. Stir in olives and raisins. Beat egg yolk slightly; stir into sausage mixture, mixing well. Carefully unfold crusts. Cut into desired shapes using 3-inch cookie cutters. Place about 2 teaspoons sausage filling on half the cutouts. Top with remaining cutouts. (Or, use round cutter, top with sausage filling and fold dough over to create half-moon shape.) Moisten fingers with water and pinch dough to seal edges. Slightly beat egg white; gently brush over tops of empanadas. Bake in 425°F oven 15 to 18 minutes or until golden brown.

*Makes 12 appetizer servings*

*Favorite recipe from* **National Pork Board**

[ **Notas** ] Empanadas are savory or sweet filled pastries similar to turnovers. Usually in the shape of a half circle or triangle, they may be deep-fried or baked. Empanadas are excellent appetizers because they can be made ahead of time. Freeze unbaked empanadas; then, bake them right before serving as directed above.

# Bell Pepper Nachos

**Nonstick cooking spray**
**1 medium green bell pepper**
**1 medium yellow or red bell pepper**
**2 Italian plum tomatoes, seeded and chopped**
**⅓ cup finely chopped onion**
**1 teaspoon chili powder**
**½ teaspoon ground cumin**
**1½ cups cooked white rice**
**½ cup (2 ounces) shredded Monterey Jack cheese**
**¼ cup chopped fresh cilantro**
**2 teaspoons jalapeño pepper sauce *or* ¼ teaspoon hot**
**pepper sauce**
**½ cup (2 ounces) shredded sharp Cheddar cheese**

[ 1 ] Spray large baking sheets with cooking spray; set aside.

[ 2 ] Cut bell peppers into 2×1½-inch strips; cut strips into bite-size triangles (each bell pepper strip should yield 2 or 3 triangles).

[ 3 ] Spray large nonstick skillet with cooking spray. Add tomatoes, onion, chili powder and cumin. Cook over medium heat 3 minutes or until onion is tender, stirring occasionally. Remove from heat. Stir in rice, Monterey Jack cheese, cilantro and pepper sauce.

[ 4 ] Top each pepper triangle with about 2 tablespoons rice mixture; sprinkle with Cheddar cheese. Place on prepared baking sheets; cover with plastic wrap. Refrigerate 30 minutes to up to 8 hours before serving.

[ 5 ] When ready to serve, preheat broiler. Remove plastic wrap. Broil nachos, 6 to 8 inches from heat, 3 to 4 minutes (or bake at 400°F 8 to 10 minutes) or until cheese is bubbly and rice is heated through. Transfer to serving plate. *Makes 8 servings*

# Mango-Lime Cooler

**2 large mangoes, peeled, seeded and cubed**
**2 cups cold water**
**1 cup ice**
**½ cup sugar**
**½ cup freshly squeezed lime juice (about 6 limes)**

Combine all ingredients in blender. Blend at high speed until smooth.
*Makes 4 servings*

# Southwestern Chili Cheese Empanadas

**¾ cup (3 ounces) finely shredded taco-flavored cheese\***
**⅓ cup diced green chiles, drained**
**1 package (15 ounces) refrigerated pie crusts**
**1 egg**
**Chili powder**

*\*If taco-flavored cheese is unavailable, toss ¾ cup shredded Colby Jack cheese with ½ teaspoon chili powder.*

[1] Combine cheese and chiles in small bowl.

[2] Unfold 1 pastry crust on floured surface. Roll into 13-inch circle. Cut dough into 16 rounds using 3-inch cookie cutter, rerolling scraps as necessary. Repeat with remaining crust to make 32 circles.

[3] Spoon 1 teaspoon cheese mixture in center of each dough round. Fold round in half, sealing edge with tines of fork.

[4] Place empanadas on waxed paper-lined baking sheets; freeze, uncovered, 1 hour or until firm. Place in resealable plastic food storage bags. Freeze up to 2 months, if desired.

[5] To complete recipe, preheat oven to 400°F. Place frozen empanadas on ungreased baking sheet. Beat egg and 1 tablespoon water in small bowl; brush on empanadas. Sprinkle with chili powder.

[6] Bake 12 to 17 minutes or until golden brown. Remove from baking sheet to wire rack to cool.          *Makes 32 appetizers*

**Serving Suggestion:** Serve empanadas with salsa and sour cream.

# Pineapple Margaritas

**⅔ cup DOLE® Pineapple Juice**
**1½ ounces tequila**
**1 ounce Triple Sec**
**Juice of 1 lemon**
**Crushed ice**

• Combine pineapple juice, tequila, Triple Sec and lemon juice in blender. Add ice; blend until slushy. Serve in frosted glasses. (Do not put salt on rim.)          *Makes 2 servings*

**Hearty Nachos**

# Hearty Nachos

**1 pound ground beef**
**1 envelope LIPTON® RECIPE SECRETS® Onion Soup Mix**
**1 can (19 ounces) black beans, rinsed and drained**
**1 cup prepared salsa**
**1 package (8½ ounces) plain tortilla chips**
**1 cup shredded Cheddar cheese (about 4 ounces)**

[ 1 ] In 12-inch nonstick skillet, brown ground beef over medium-high heat; drain.

[ 2 ] Stir in soup mix, black beans and salsa. Bring to a boil over high heat. Reduce heat to low and simmer 5 minutes or until heated through.

[ 3 ] Arrange tortilla chips on serving platter. Spread beef mixture over chips; sprinkle with Cheddar cheese. Top with sliced green onions, sliced pitted ripe olives, chopped tomato and chopped cilantro.

*Makes 8 servings*

# Mexican Chili Walnuts

**2 egg whites, slightly beaten**
**1 tablespoon chili powder**
**2 teaspoons ground cumin**
**2 teaspoons salt**
**1½ teaspoons ground cayenne pepper**
**4 cups (1 pound) California walnut halves and pieces**

Coat large shallow baking pan with nonstick vegetable spray. Mix egg whites with spices; stir in walnuts and coat thoroughly. Spread in prepared pan. Bake in 350°F oven 15 to 18 minutes or until dry and crisp. Cool completely before serving. *Makes 4 cups*

**Note:** Best if made at least one day ahead. Flavors intensify overnight. Store in sealed container.

**Microwave Directions:** Microwave on high in 4 or 5 batches for 2 to 3 minutes each, until dry and crisp. Cool completely.

*Favorite recipe from* **Walnut Marketing Board**

**Cheesy Quesadillas**

# Cheesy Quesadillas

½ **pound ground beef**
1 **medium onion, chopped**
¼ **teaspoon salt**
1 **can (4½ ounces) chopped green chilies, drained**
1 **jar (1 pound 10 ounces) RAGÚ® Robusto!® Pasta Sauce**
8 **(6½-inch) flour tortillas**
1 **tablespoon olive oil**
2 **cups shredded Cheddar and/or mozzarella cheese
   (about 8 ounces)**

[ 1 ] Preheat oven to 400°F. In 12-inch skillet, brown ground beef with onion and salt over medium-high heat; drain. Stir in chilies and ½ cup Ragú Pasta Sauce; set aside.

[ 2 ] Meanwhile, evenly brush one side of 4 tortillas with half of the olive oil. On cookie sheets, arrange tortillas, oil-side down. Evenly top with ½ of the cheese, beef filling, then remaining cheese. Top with remaining 4 tortillas, then brush tops with remaining oil.

[ 3 ] Bake 10 minutes or until cheese is melted. To serve, cut each quesadilla into 4 wedges. Serve with remaining sauce, heated.

*Makes 4 servings*

# [ Notas ] 
Quesadillas are simply tortilla sandwiches. One of Mexico's most popular snacks, they are made from flour tortillas topped with shredded cheese, such as Monterey Jack or Chihuahua. Then they are folded into half moons and toasted on a griddle or in a skillet until the cheese melts. An alternate method is to place the filling ingredients on a large tortilla. The filling is then topped with a second tortilla, and the quesadilla is toasted on a griddle. This large quesadilla is cut into wedges to serve. Quesadillas are a versatile party food. They can be made up to a day ahead and refrigerated; reheat them on a baking sheet in a 375°F oven for 15 minutes.

Chicken Empanadas

# Chicken Empanadas

**4 ounces cream cheese**
**2 tablespoons chopped fresh cilantro**
**2 tablespoons salsa**
**½ teaspoon salt**
**½ teaspoon ground cumin**
**¼ teaspoon garlic powder**
**1 cup finely chopped cooked chicken**
**1 box (15 ounces) refrigerated pie crusts**
   **(two 11-inch rounds), at room temperature**
**1 egg, beaten**
**Additional salsa (optional)**

[ 1 ] Heat cream cheese in small heavy saucepan over low heat; cook and stir until melted. Add cilantro, salsa, salt, cumin and garlic powder; stir until smooth. Stir in chicken; remove from heat.

[ 2 ] Roll out pie crust dough slightly on lightly floured surface. Cut dough with 3-inch round cookie or biscuit cutter. Reroll dough scraps and cut enough additional to make 20 rounds.

[ 3 ] Preheat oven to 425°F. Line 2 baking sheets with parchment paper or foil. Place about 2 teaspoons chicken mixture in center of each round. Brush edges lightly with water. Pull one side of dough over filling to form half circle; pinch edges to seal.

[ 4 ] Place 10 empanadas on prepared baking sheets; brush lightly with egg. Bake 16 to 18 minutes or until lightly browned. Serve with salsa.                              *Makes 10 appetizer servings*

**Tip:** Empanadas can be prepared ahead of time and frozen. Simply wrap unbaked empanadas in plastic wrap and freeze. To bake, unwrap and follow directions in step 4. Bake 18 to 20 minutes.

# Cheesy Chorizo Wedges

**Red & Green Salsa (recipe follows)**
**1 cup (4 ounces) shredded mild Cheddar cheese**
**1 cup (4 ounces) shredded Monterey Jack cheese**
**8 ounces chorizo**
**3 flour tortillas (10-inch diameter)**

[ 1 ] Prepare Red & Green Salsa.

[ 2 ] Preheat oven to 450°F. Combine cheeses in small bowl.

[ 3 ] Remove and discard casing from chorizo. Heat medium skillet over high heat until hot. Reduce heat to medium. Crumble chorizo into skillet. Brown 6 to 8 minutes, stirring to separate meat. Remove with slotted spoon; drain on paper towels.

[ 4 ] Place tortillas on baking sheets. Divide chorizo evenly among tortillas, leaving ½ inch of edges of tortillas uncovered. Sprinkle cheese mixture over top.

[ 5 ] Bake 8 to 10 minutes until edges are crisp and golden and cheese is bubbly and melted.

[ 6 ] Transfer to serving plates; cut each tortilla into 6 wedges. Serve with Red & Green Salsa. *Makes 6 to 8 servings*

## Red & Green Salsa

**1 small red bell pepper**
**¼ cup coarsely chopped fresh cilantro**
**3 green onions, cut into thin slices**
**2 fresh jalapeño peppers,* seeded, minced**
**2 tablespoons fresh lime juice**
**1 clove garlic, minced**
**¼ teaspoon salt**

*Jalapeño peppers can sting and irritate the skin. Wear rubber gloves when handling peppers and do not touch your eyes.*

[ 1 ] Cut bell pepper lengthwise in half; remove and discard seeds and veins. Cut halves lengthwise into thin slivers; cut slivers crosswise into halves.

[ 2 ] Mix all ingredients in small bowl. Let stand, covered, at room temperature 1 to 2 hours to blend flavors. *Makes 1 cup*

# Margaritas

**8 ounces tequila**
**4 ounces Triple Sec**
**8 ounces fresh lime juice**
**¼ cup sugar**
  **Crushed ice**
  **Additional lime juice (for glass rims, optional)**
  **Coarse or kosher salt (for glass rims, optional)**

In blender jar, mix tequila, Triple Sec, lime juice, sugar and crushed ice until frothy. Dip rim of glass in lime juice, then in salt, if desired. Fill with margarita mixture. *Makes 4 servings*

**Meal Idea:** Serve in an iced pitcher with all your favorite Mexican entrées or appetizers. Great for parties.

**Variations:** Use about 1 cup (8 ounces) sweet-and-sour bar mix in place of fresh lime juice and sugar. To make Strawberry Margaritas, blend in about 1 to 1½ cups fresh strawberries.

*Favorite recipe from* **Lawrys® Foods**

[ **Notas** ] The margarita is the most common tequila-based cocktail. To most people, a Margarita is served with salt on the rim of the glass. Opinions differ whether or not salt adds to the flavor of the drink or whether it hides an inferior flavor. To please everyone, dip only half the glass in salt.

California Quesadillas

# California Quesadillas

1 small ripe avocado
2 packages (3 ounces each) cream cheese, softened
3 tablespoons *Frank's® RedHot®* Original Cayenne
  Pepper Sauce
¼ cup minced fresh cilantro leaves
16 (6-inch) flour tortillas (2 packages)
1 cup (4 ounces) shredded Cheddar or Monterey Jack
  cheese
½ cup finely chopped green onions
  Sour cream (optional)

[ 1 ] Halve avocado and remove pit. Scoop out flesh into food processor or bowl of electric mixer. Add cream cheese and **Frank's RedHot** Sauce. Cover and process or beat until smooth. Add cilantro; process or beat until well blended. Spread rounded tablespoon avocado mixture onto each tortilla. Sprinkle half the tortillas with cheese and onions, dividing evenly. Top with remaining tortillas; press gently.

[ 2 ] Place tortillas on oiled grid. Grill over medium coals 5 minutes or until cheese melts and tortillas are lightly browned, turning once. Cut into triangles. Serve with sour cream, if desired. Garnish as desired.

*Makes 8 appetizer servings*

**Note:** You may serve avocado mixture as a dip with tortilla chips.

[ **Notas** ] Avocados from Mexico have dark rough skin. When ripe, the skin is almost black. Firm avocados require additional ripening at home. To speed up the ripening process, put avocados in a paper bag. Store them at room temperature for 2 to 3 days until they yield to gentle palm pressure, then use promptly or refrigerate. To prevent the cut surfaces of the avocado from darkening, squeeze lemon juice over cut surfaces.

# Tortilla Dishes

## Triangle Tostadas

2 large (burrito size) flour tortillas
  Vegetable oil
1 package (about 1 pound) lean ground pork
1 package (1 ounce) LAWRY'S® Taco Spices & Seasonings
⅔ cup water
1 can (16 ounces) refried beans, warmed

**TOPPINGS**
  **Shredded lettuce and cheese, chopped tomatoes**

Preheat oven to 400°F. Cut each tortilla into quarters, forming
4 triangles. Place triangles in single layer on baking sheet. Brush each
side of triangle lightly with oil. Bake for 4 to 5 minutes or until golden
brown and crispy; let cool. Meanwhile, in large skillet, brown ground
pork over medium high heat until crumbly; drain fat. Stir in Taco
Spices & Seasonings and water. Bring to a boil; reduce heat to low
and cook, uncovered for 7 minutes or until pork is thoroughly cooked,
stirring occasionally. To assemble tostadas, evenly divide and spread
refried beans on each tortilla triangle. Spread about ¼ cup seasoned
pork on top of beans. Top with shredded lettuce, cheese and
tomatoes, as desired.                              *Makes 8 tostadas*

**Variations:** Cut each tortilla into 8 pieces and make mini appetizer
tostadas. For additional toppings, try sliced black olives, sour cream,
guacamole, salsa or jalapeños.

Cheesy Chicken Enchiladas

# Cheesy Chicken Enchiladas

**¼ cup (½ stick) butter**
**1 cup chopped onion**
**2 cloves garlic, minced**
**¼ cup all-purpose flour**
**1 cup chicken broth**
**4 ounces cream cheese, softened**
**2 cups (8 ounces) shredded Mexican cheese blend, divided**
**1 cup shredded cooked chicken**
**1 can (7 ounces) diced mild green chiles, drained**
**½ cup diced pimientos**
**6 (8-inch) flour tortillas, warmed**
**¼ cup chopped fresh cilantro**
**¾ cup prepared salsa**

[ 1 ] Preheat oven to 350°F. Spray 13×9-inch baking dish with nonstick cooking spray.

[ 2 ] Melt butter in medium saucepan over medium heat. Add onion and garlic; cook and stir until onion is tender. Add flour; cook and stir 1 minute. Gradually whisk in chicken broth; cook and stir 2 to 3 minutes or until slightly thickened. Add cream cheese; stir until melted. Stir in ½ cup shredded cheese, chicken, chiles and pimientos.

[ 3 ] Spoon about ⅓ cup mixture onto each tortilla. Roll up and place seam side down in prepared baking dish. Pour remaining mixture over enchiladas; sprinkle with remaining 1½ cups shredded cheese.

[ 4 ] Bake 20 minutes or until bubbly and lightly browned. Sprinkle with cilantro and serve with salsa. *Makes 6 servings*

Chipotle Taco Filling

# Chipotle Taco Filling

2 pounds ground beef
2 cans (about 15 ounces each) pinto beans, rinsed
    and drained
2 cups chopped onions
1 can (about 14½ ounces) diced tomatoes with peppers
    and onions, drained
2 chipotle peppers in adobo sauce, mashed
1 tablespoon sugar
1 tablespoon beef bouillon granules
1½ teaspoons ground cumin
    Taco shells or flour tortillas
    Shredded lettuce, salsa, shredded Mexican blend
    cheese and sour cream

## SLOW COOKER DIRECTIONS

[ 1 ] Brown beef in large nonstick skillet over medium-high heat, stirring to break up meat. Drain fat.

[ 2 ] Combine beef, beans, onions, tomatoes, peppers, sugar, bouillon and cumin in slow cooker. Cover; cook on LOW 4 hours or on HIGH 2 hours.

[ 3 ] Serve filling in taco shells. Top with lettuce, salsa, cheese and sour cream.                    *Makes 8 cups filling*

[ **Notas** ] Chipotle peppers are dried smoked jalapeño peppers. They are often packed in adobo sauce which is a dark red sauce or paste made from ground chiles, herbs and vinegar. Chipotle peppers in adobo sauce can be found in the Mexican foods section of supermarkets. They can add a very hot spicy flavor to a dish.

Southwestern Enchiladas

# Southwestern Enchiladas

**1 can (10 ounces) enchilada sauce**
**2 packages (about 6 ounces each) refrigerated**
**fully cooked steak strips**
**4 (8-inch) flour tortillas**
**½ cup canned condensed nacho cheese soup**
***or* ½ cup chile-flavored cheese spread**
**1½ cups (6 ounces) shredded Mexican cheese blend**

*Fully cooked steak strips can be found in the refrigerated prepared meats
section of the supermarket.*

[ 1 ] Preheat oven to 350°F. Spread half of enchilada sauce in 9-inch
glass baking dish; set aside.

[ 2 ] Divide steak evenly down center of each tortilla. Top with
2 tablespoons cheese soup. Roll up tortillas; place seam side down
in baking dish. Pour remaining enchilada sauce evenly over tortillas.
Sprinkle with cheese. Bake 20 to 25 minutes or until heated through.

*Makes 4 servings*

# Easy Family Burritos

**1 boneless beef chuck shoulder roast (2 to 3 pounds)**
**1 jar (24 ounces) *or* 2 jars (16 ounces each) salsa**
**Flour tortillas**

### SLOW COOKER DIRECTIONS

[ 1 ] Place roast in slow cooker; top with salsa. Cover; cook on LOW
8 to 10 hours.

[ 2 ] Remove beef from slow cooker. Shred meat with 2 forks. Return
to slow cooker. Cover; cook 1 to 2 hours or until heated through.

[ 3 ] Serve shredded meat wrapped in warm tortillas.

*Makes 8 servings*

Chicken Enchilada Skillet Casserole

# Chicken Enchilada Skillet Casserole

**1 bag (16 ounces) BIRDS EYE® frozen Farm Fresh Mixtures Broccoli, Corn & Red Peppers**
**3 cups shredded cooked chicken**
**1 can (16 ounces) diced tomatoes, undrained**
**1 package (1¼ ounces) taco seasoning mix**
**1 cup shredded Monterey Jack cheese**
**8 ounces tortilla chips**

• In large skillet, combine vegetables, chicken, tomatoes and seasoning mix; bring to boil over medium-high heat.

• Cover; cook 4 minutes or until vegetables are cooked and mixture is heated through.

• Sprinkle with cheese; cover and cook 2 minutes more or until cheese is melted.

• Serve with chips.  *Makes 4 servings*

# Chicken and Black Bean Soft Tacos

**1 package (10) ORTEGA® Soft Taco Dinner Kit (flour tortillas, taco seasoning mix and taco sauce)**
**1 tablespoon vegetable oil**
**1 pound (3 to 4) boneless, skinless chicken breast halves, cut into 2-inch strips**
**1 medium onion, chopped**
**1 can (15 ounces) black beans, drained**
**¾ cup whole kernel corn**
**½ cup water**
**2 tablespoons lime juice**

**HEAT** oil in large skillet over medium-high heat. Add chicken and onion; cook 4 to 5 minutes or until chicken is no longer pink in center. Stir in taco seasoning mix, beans, corn, water and lime juice. Bring to a boil. Reduce heat to low; cook, stirring occasionally, 5 to 6 minutes or until mixture is thickened.

**REMOVE** tortillas from outer plastic pouch. Microwave using HIGH (100%) power 10 to 15 seconds or until warm.

**FILL** each tortilla with ½ cup chicken mixture. Serve with taco sauce.

*Makes 10 tacos*

**Tostada**

# Tostadas

Spiced Meat Filling (recipe follows)
1 can (about 15 ounces) refried beans
8 (6- or 7-inch) crisp-fried corn tortillas
2 cups shredded lettuce
1 cup (4 ounces) shredded Cheddar or Monterey Jack
   cheese
1 large avocado, peeled, pitted and sliced
2 tomatoes, cut into wedges or chopped
1 small onion, thinly sliced crosswise, separated into rings
1 cup salsa or picante sauce
Cilantro sprigs for garnish

[ 1 ] Prepare Spiced Meat Filling; keep warm.

[ 2 ] Heat refried beans in large skillet. To assemble each tostada,
place 1 tortilla on dinner plate and spread with about ¼ cup refried
beans. Top with meat filling, lettuce, cheese, avocado, tomatoes
and onion. Garnish with salsa and cilantro.      *Makes 8 tostadas*

## Spiced Meat Filling

½ pound ground beef
¼ pound ground pork
½ cup chopped onion
1 clove garlic, minced
1 fresh or canned jalapeño pepper,* seeded and minced
½ cup canned tomatoes, drained and finely chopped
1 tablespoon cider vinegar
1 teaspoon brown sugar
1 teaspoon chili powder
¼ teaspoon salt
¼ teaspoon ground cumin
¼ teaspoon dried oregano
⅛ teaspoon ground cinnamon

*Jalapeño peppers can sting and irritate the skin. Wear rubber gloves when
handling peppers and do not touch your eyes.*

*continued on page 35*

**Turkey Enchiladas**

*Spiced Meat Filling, continued*

[ 1 ] Crumble beef and pork into large skillet; cook and stir over medium-high heat until browned. Add onion, garlic and jalapeño pepper. Reduce heat to medium; cook until onion is tender. Drain and discard pan drippings. Add remaining ingredients.

[ 2 ] Simmer, stirring occasionally, 15 minutes or until most of liquid has evaporated.

# Turkey Enchiladas

**1 package (16 ounces) JENNIE-O TURKEY STORE®**
**SO EASY Turkey Breast Chunks in Alfredo Sauce**
**1 small onion, chopped**
**1 can (15 ounces) green or red enchilada sauce**
**1 container (8 ounces) sour cream**
**Vegetable oil**
**8 (6-inch) white or yellow corn tortillas**
**1 cup shredded Monterey Jack & Cheddar cheeses**
**(optional)**
**Prepared salsa (optional)**

Preheat oven to 350°F.

In large bowl, combine turkey in Alfredo sauce and onion. In another bowl, combine enchilada sauce and sour cream. Add about ½ cup enchilada sauce to turkey mixture.

To soften corn tortillas, place small amount of oil in skillet. Heat oil until hot. Carefully dip each tortilla in oil, 5 seconds per side, to soften. Drain tortillas on paper towels.

Spread small amount of enchilada sauce over bottom of 13×9-inch baking dish. Evenly divide turkey mixture down center of each tortilla. Roll tortillas up and place seam side down in baking dish. Pour remaining enchilada sauce over tortillas. Sprinkle with cheese, if desired.

Bake 30 to 35 minutes or until hot. Top with salsa, if desired.

*Makes 4 servings*

# Pork Burritos

**1 boneless fresh pork butt roast (about 2½ pounds)**
**1 cup chopped white onion**
**1 carrot, sliced**
**1 clove garlic, minced**
**½ teaspoon salt**
**½ teaspoon ground cumin**
**½ teaspoon coriander seeds, lightly crushed**
  **Water**
  **Fresh Tomato Salsa (page 37)**
**12 flour tortillas (8-inch diameter)**
 **2 cups canned refried beans, warmed**
 **2 medium avocados, peeled, diced**
 **1 cup (4 ounces) shredded Monterey Jack cheese**

[ 1 ] Place pork, onion, carrot, garlic, salt, cumin and coriander seeds in 5-quart Dutch oven. Add just enough water to cover pork. Bring to a boil over high heat. Reduce heat to low. Cover; simmer 2 to 2½ hours until pork is tender.

[ 2 ] Prepare Fresh Tomato Salsa.

[ 3 ] Preheat oven to 350°F. Remove pork from Dutch oven; set aside. Strain cooking liquid through cheesecloth-lined sieve; reserve ½ cup liquid.

[ 4 ] Place pork on rack in roasting pan. Roast 40 to 45 minutes until well browned, turning once. Let stand until cool enough to handle.

[ 5 ] Trim and discard outer fat from pork. Using 2 forks, pull pork into coarse shreds. Combine pork and reserved cooking liquid in medium skillet. Heat over medium heat 5 minutes or until meat is hot, stirring frequently.

[ 6 ] Soften and warm tortillas.

[ 7 ] Spread about 2½ tablespoons beans on bottom half of 1 tortilla. Top with pork, salsa, diced avocado and cheese. Fold right edge of tortilla up over filling; fold bottom edge over filling, then loosely roll up, leaving left end of burrito open.    *Makes 6 servings*

## Fresh Tomato Salsa

**1 medium tomato, finely chopped**
**¼ cup coarsely chopped fresh cilantro**
**2 tablespoons finely chopped white onion**
**1 fresh jalapeño pepper,* seeded and minced**
**1 tablespoon fresh lime juice**

*Jalapeño peppers can sting and irritate the skin. Wear rubber gloves when handling peppers and do not touch your eyes.*

Combine all ingredients in small bowl; mix well. Let stand, covered, at room temperature 1 to 2 hours to blend flavors.

*Makes about ¾ cup*

## Taco Two-Zies

**1 pound ground beef**
**2 packages (1 ounce each) LAWRY'S® Taco Spices**
**& Seasonings**
**⅔ cup water**
**1 can (1 pound 14 ounces) refried beans, warmed**
**10 small flour tortillas (fajita size), warmed to soften**
**10 jumbo size taco shells, heated according to package**
**directions**

**TACO TOPPINGS**
**Shredded lettuce, shredded Cheddar cheese and chopped tomatoes**

In large skillet, brown ground beef over medium high heat until crumbly; drain fat. Stir in 1 package Taco Spices & Seasonings and water. Bring to a boil; reduce heat to low and cook, uncovered, 10 minutes, stirring occasionally. In medium bowl, mix together beans and remaining package Taco Spices & Seasonings. Spread about ⅓ cup seasoned beans all the way to edges of each flour tortilla. Place a taco shell on center of each bean-tortilla and fold edges up around shell, lightly pressing to 'stick' tortilla to shell. Fill each taco with about 3 tablespoons taco meat. Top with your choice of taco toppings.

*Makes 10 tacos*

**Variations:** May use lean ground turkey, chicken or pork in place of ground beef. May use LAWRY'S® Chicken Taco Spices & Seasonings or Lawry's® Hot Taco Spices & Seasonings instead of Taco Spices & Seasonings.

**Black Bean Garnacha**

# Black Bean Garnachas

**1 can (14½ ounces) DEL MONTE® Diced Tomatoes**
**    with Garlic & Onion**
**1 can (15 ounces) black or pinto beans, drained**
**2 cloves garlic, minced**
**1 to 2 teaspoons minced jalapeño peppers (optional)**
**½ teaspoon ground cumin**
**1 cup cubed grilled chicken**
**4 flour tortillas**
**½ cup (2 ounces) shredded sharp Cheddar cheese**

[ 1 ] Combine undrained tomatoes, beans, garlic, jalapeño peppers and cumin in large skillet. Cook over medium-high heat 5 to 7 minutes or until thickened, stirring occasionally. Stir in chicken. Season with salt and pepper, if desired.

[ 2 ] Arrange tortillas in single layer on grill over medium coals. Spread about ¾ cup chicken mixture over each tortilla. Top with cheese.

[ 3 ] Cook about 3 minutes or until bottoms of tortillas are browned and cheese is melted. Top with shredded lettuce, diced avocado and sliced jalapeño peppers, if desired. *Makes 4 servings*

**Variation:** Prepare chicken mixture as directed above. Place a tortilla in a dry skillet over medium heat. Spread with about ¾ cup chicken mixture; top with 2 tablespoons cheese. Cover and cook about 3 minutes or until bottom of tortilla is browned and cheese is melted. Repeat with remaining tortillas.

[ **Notas** ] Keep cooked chicken on hand for quick-to-fix Mexican dishes. Either purchase a rotisserie chicken or look for fully cooked chicken products in the prepared meats section of the supermarket. Cooked chicken pieces are terrific for salad toppings and taco, enchilada and quesadilla fillings.

**Enticing Enchiladas**

# Enticing Enchiladas

1 tablespoon vegetable oil
1 green or red bell pepper, chopped
½ cup chopped onion
4 cloves garlic, minced
1 package **JENNIE-O TURKEY STORE**® Lean Ground Turkey
1 tablespoon Mexican seasoning or chili powder
2 cans (10 ounces) mild enchilada sauce, divided
2 cups (8 ounces) shredded Mexican cheese blend or Monterey Jack cheese, divided
12 (7-inch) soft flour tortillas or flavored flour tortillas
1 cup shredded lettuce
½ cup diced tomato
Ripe avocado slices (optional)

Heat oven to 375°F. Heat oil in large skillet over medium heat. Add bell pepper, onion and garlic; cook 5 minutes, stirring occasionally. Crumble turkey into skillet; sprinkle with seasoning. Cook about 8 minutes or until no longer pink, stirring occasionally. Stir in ½ cup enchilada sauce. Remove from heat; stir in 1 cup cheese. Spread ½ cup enchilada sauce over bottom of 13×9-inch baking dish. Spoon about ⅓ cup turkey mixture down center of each tortilla. Fold bottom of tortilla up over filling, fold in sides and roll up. Place, seam side down, in prepared dish. Spoon remaining enchilada sauce evenly over enchiladas. Cover with foil; bake 20 minutes. Sprinkle with remaining 1 cup cheese. Return to oven; bake, uncovered, 10 minutes or until cheese is melted and sauce is bubbly. Garnish with lettuce and tomato. Top with avocado, if desired.          *Makes 6 servings*

# Mexican Meats & Poultry

## Green Chile-Chicken Casserole

**4 cups shredded cooked chicken**
**1½ cups green enchilada sauce**
**1 can (10¾ ounces) condensed cream of chicken soup,**
**undiluted**
**1 container (8 ounces) sour cream**
**1 can (4 ounces) diced mild green chiles**
**½ cup vegetable oil**
**12 (6-inch) corn tortillas**
**1½ cups (6 ounces) shredded Colby-Jack cheese, divided**

[1] Preheat oven to 325°F. Grease 13×9-inch casserole.

[2] Combine chicken, enchilada sauce, soup, sour cream and chiles in large skillet. Cook and stir over medium-high heat until warm.

[3] Heat oil in separate deep skillet. Fry tortillas just until soft; drain on paper towels. Place 4 tortillas on bottom of prepared casserole. Layer with one third of chicken mixture and ½ cup cheese. Repeat layers twice.

[4] Bake 15 to 20 minutes or until cheese is melted and casserole is heated through. *Makes 6 servings*

**Variation:** Shredded Mexican cheese blend can be substituted for Colby-Jack cheese.

**Tamale Pie**

# Tamale Pie

**1 pound ground beef**
**1 can (about 14 ounces) diced tomatoes**
**1 package (10 ounces) frozen corn, thawed**
**1 can (4 ounces) sliced black olives, drained**
**1 package (1¼ ounces) taco seasoning mix**
**1 package (6 ounces) corn muffin mix, plus ingredients**
   **to prepare mix**
**¼ cup (1 ounce) shredded Cheddar cheese**
**1 green onion, thinly sliced**

[ 1 ] Preheat oven to 400°F. Brown beef in large skillet 6 to 8 minutes over medium-high heat, stirring to break up meat. Drain fat.

[ 2 ] Add tomatoes, corn, olives and seasoning mix to beef. Bring to a boil over medium-high heat, stirring constantly. Pour mixture into deep 9-inch pie plate; smooth top with spatula.

[ 3 ] Prepare corn muffin mix according to package directions. Spread evenly over beef mixture. Bake 8 to 10 minutes or until golden brown. Sprinkle with cheese and onion. Let stand 10 minutes before serving.

*Makes 6 servings*

**Serving Suggestion:** Serve with papaya wedges sprinkled with lime juice.

[ Notas ] Traditional tamales are corn husks or banana leaves stuffed with corn dough and savory fillings and then steamed. This delicious tamale pie is a quick way to capture some of the flavors of tamales.

# Flautas with Chicken Filling

**6 boneless skinless chicken breasts (about 1½ pounds)**
**1 can (4 ounces) diced green chiles, drained**
**½ cup water**
**½ teaspoon ground cumin**
**⅛ teaspoon salt**
**Fresh Tomato Salsa (page 37)**
**1 cup Classic Guacamole (page 3) or prepared guacamole**
**12 corn tortillas (6-inch diameter)**
**Vegetable oil**
**1 cup (4 ounces) shredded Monterey Jack cheese**
**½ cup sour cream**

[ 1 ] Combine chicken, chiles, water, cumin and salt in large skillet. Bring to a boil over medium-high heat. Reduce heat to low. Cover; simmer 15 to 20 minutes until chicken is tender. Remove chicken; let stand until cool enough to handle. Reserve chile mixture.

[ 2 ] Meanwhile, prepare Fresh Tomato Salsa and Classic Guacamole.

[ 3 ] Cut chicken across the grain into thin slices. Warm corn tortillas.

[ 4 ] For each flauta, overlap 2 tortillas by about half of each tortilla. Spoon one-eighth of chicken down center. Top with one-eighth of reserved chile mixture. Roll up as tightly as possible.

[ 5 ] Preheat oven to 250°F. Heat 1 inch oil in deep, heavy skillet over medium-high heat to 375°F; adjust heat to maintain temperature. Line baking sheet with paper towels.

[ 6 ] Fry flautas, 1 or 2 at a time, in oil, holding closed with tongs during first 30 seconds to prevent flautas from unrolling. Fry 2 minutes or until crisp and golden on all sides, turning occasionally. Drain on paper towels. Keep warm in oven on prepared baking sheet.

[ 7 ] Serve flautas with cheese, sour cream, Fresh Tomato Salsa and Classic Guacamole.                    *Makes 4 to 6 servings*

# Stuffed Mexican Pizza Pie

**1 pound ground beef**
**1 large onion, chopped**
**1 large green bell pepper, chopped**
**1½ cups UNCLE BEN'S® Instant Rice**
**2 cans (14½ ounces each) Mexican-style stewed tomatoes, undrained**
**⅔ cup water**
**2 cups (8 ounces) shredded Mexican-style seasoned Monterey Jack-Colby cheese blend, divided**
**1 package (10 ounces) refrigerated pizza crust dough**

[ 1 ] Preheat oven to 425°F. Spray 13×9-inch baking pan with cooking spray; set aside.

[ 2 ] Spray large nonstick skillet with nonstick cooking spray; heat over high heat until hot. Add beef, onion and bell pepper; cook and stir 5 minutes or until meat is no longer pink.

[ 3 ] Add rice, stewed tomatoes and water. Bring to a boil. Pour beef mixture into prepared baking pan. Sprinkle with 1¼ cups cheese and stir until blended.

[ 4 ] Unroll pizza crust dough on work surface. Place dough in one even layer over mixture in baking pan. Cut 6 to 8 slits in dough with sharp knife. Bake 10 minutes or until crust is lightly browned. Sprinkle top of crust with remaining ¾ cup cheese; continue baking 4 minutes or until cheese is melted and crust is deep golden brown.

[ 5 ] Let stand 5 minutes before cutting.                    *Makes 6 servings*

**Cilantro-Lime Chicken**

# Cilantro-Lime Chicken

**1 pound boneless skinless chicken breasts**
**2 small onions**
**1 large lime**
**2 tablespoons canola oil**
**1 or 2 small green or red jalapeño peppers,* seeded**
**    and sliced**
**1 small piece fresh ginger (1 inch long), peeled**
**    and thinly sliced**
**2 tablespoons chopped fresh cilantro**
**2 tablespoons soy sauce**
**1 to 2 teaspoons sugar**
**    Hot cooked rice**
**    Cilantro sprigs, grated lime peel and red jalapeño**
**        pepper* strips**

*Jalapeño peppers can sting and irritate the skin. Wear rubber gloves when handling peppers and do not touch your eyes.*

[ 1 ] Cut each chicken breast half into 8 pieces. Cut each onion into 8 wedges.

[ 2 ] Remove 3 strips of peel from lime with vegetable peeler. Cut lime peel into very fine shreds. Juice lime; measure 2 tablespoons juice. Set aside.

[ 3 ] Heat wok or large skillet over medium-high heat 1 minute or until hot. Drizzle oil into wok and heat 30 seconds. Add chicken, jalapeño and ginger; stir-fry about 3 minutes or until chicken is no longer pink in center. Reduce heat to medium.

[ 4 ] Add onions; stir-fry 5 minutes.

[ 5 ] Add lime peel, juice and chopped cilantro; stir-fry 1 minute. Add soy sauce and sugar; stir-fry until heated through. Transfer to serving dish. Serve with rice. Garnish with cilantro, lime peel and red jalapeño pepper.                     *Makes 4 servings*

Chicken Fajitas

# Chicken Fajitas

1 tablespoon vegetable oil
1 large green bell pepper, thinly sliced
1 large red bell pepper, thinly sliced
1 large onion, thinly sliced
1 clove garlic, minced
4 boneless skinless chicken breast halves (about
    1 pound), cut into ½-inch strips
½ teaspoon dried oregano
2 tablespoons dry white wine or water
  Salt and black pepper
8 (8-inch) flour tortillas
  Guacamole

[ 1 ] Heat oil in large skillet over medium-high heat. Add bell peppers, onion and garlic. Cook 3 to 4 minutes or until crisp-tender, stirring occasionally. Remove vegetables with slotted spoon; set aside.

[ 2 ] Add chicken and oregano to skillet. Cook 4 minutes or until chicken is no longer pink in center, stirring occasionally.

[ 3 ] Return vegetables to skillet. Add wine. Season with salt and black pepper to taste; cover. Continue cooking 2 minutes or until thoroughly heated.

[ 4 ] Meanwhile, stack tortillas and wrap in foil. Heat in 350°F oven 10 minutes or until warm. Fill tortillas with chicken mixture; serve with guacamole. *Makes 4 servings*

[ **Notas** ] Traditional fajitas are prepared by marinating beef skirt steak in oil, lime juice, garlic and ground red pepper before grilling. The steak is cut into thin strips and rolled in flour tortillas. Fajitas now often include grilled bell peppers and onions. They are served with sour cream, guacamole and salsa. Sometimes the dish is prepared with beef flank steak, chicken strips or shrimp.

Arroz con Pollo

# Arroz con Pollo

    4 slices bacon
1½ pounds (about 6) boneless, skinless chicken breasts
    1 cup (1 small) chopped onion
    1 cup (1 small) chopped green bell pepper
    2 large cloves garlic, finely chopped
    2 cups uncooked long-grain white rice
    1 jar (16 ounces) ORTEGA® Salsa (any flavor)
1¾ cups (14½-ounce can) chicken broth
    1 cup (8-ounce can) tomato sauce
    1 teaspoon salt
½ teaspoon ground cumin
    Chopped fresh parsley

**COOK** bacon in large saucepan over medium-high heat until crispy; remove from saucepan. Crumble bacon; set aside. Add chicken to saucepan; cook, turning frequently, for 5 to 7 minutes or until golden on both sides. Remove from saucepan; keep warm. Discard all but 2 tablespoons drippings from saucepan.

**ADD** onion, bell pepper and garlic; cook for 3 to 4 minutes or until crisp-tender. Add rice; cook for 2 to 3 minutes. Stir in salsa, chicken broth, tomato sauce, salt and cumin. Bring to a boil. Place chicken over rice mixture; reduce heat to low. Cover. Cook for 20 to 25 minutes or until most of moisture is absorbed and chicken is no longer pink in center. Sprinkle with bacon and parsley.

*Makes 4 to 6 servings*

Carne Asada

# Carne Asada

1 beef flank or round tip steak (1½ to 1¾ pounds)
½ cup lime juice
6 cloves garlic, chopped
1 teaspoon black pepper
1 large green bell pepper, cut lengthwise into 1-inch strips
1 tablespoon olive oil
8 corn tortillas, warmed
   Tomato salsa

[ 1 ] Combine steak, lime juice, garlic and black pepper in resealable plastic food storage bag; seal. Refrigerate 1 to 2 hours, turning at least once to marinate steak evenly.

[ 2 ] Preheat broiler. Remove steak from bag and place on broiler pan. Sprinkle with salt to taste. Brush peppers with oil. Broil steak 6 to 9 minutes per side for medium rare to medium, turning once. Add pepper strips to broiler pan while turning steak.

[ 3 ] Transfer steak to cutting board; slice across the grain into thin strips. Place on warm tortillas. Top with pepper strips and salsa. Serve immediately. *Makes 4 servings*

# Chile Rellenos Casserole

1½ cups (6 ounces) shredded Monterey Jack *or* cheddar
      cheese, *divided*
1 can (4 ounces) ORTEGA® Diced Green Chiles
2 tablespoons all-purpose flour
1½ cups milk
3 eggs, lightly beaten

**GARNISH SUGGESTIONS**
      ORTEGA Salsa-Thick & Chunky, sour cream, sliced ripe
      olives, chopped green onions

**PREHEAT** oven to 325°F. Lightly grease 8-inch-square baking dish.

**SPRINKLE** ¾ *cup* cheese onto bottom of prepared baking dish. Top with chiles and *remaining* cheese. Place flour in medium bowl. Gradually add milk, stirring until smooth. Stir in eggs; pour mixture over cheese.

**BAKE** for 45 to 50 minutes or until knife inserted in center comes out clean. Let stand for 10 minutes.

**SERVE** with salsa and desired toppings. *Makes 8 servings*

Mexican Hot Pot

# Mexican Hot Pot

1 tablespoon canola oil
½ pound ground beef
1 medium onion, sliced
3 cloves garlic, minced
2 teaspoons red pepper flakes
2 teaspoons dried oregano
1 teaspoon ground cumin
1 can (28 ounces) whole tomatoes, chopped, undrained
2 cups whole kernel corn
1 can (about 15 ounces) chickpeas, rinsed and drained
1 can (about 15 ounces) pinto beans, rinsed and drained
1 cup water
6 cups shredded iceberg lettuce

[ 1 ] Heat oil in large saucepan over medium-high heat. Add ground beef, onion and garlic; cook and stir 5 minutes. Add red pepper flakes, oregano and cumin; mix well.

[ 2 ] Stir in tomatoes with liquid, corn, chickpeas, pinto beans and water; bring to a boil over high heat.

[ 3 ] Reduce heat to medium-low; cover and simmer 15 minutes. Top individual servings with 1 cup shredded lettuce. Serve hot.

*Makes 6 servings*

[ Notas ] Beans are the staple of Mexican cooking. Beans and rice are served at almost every meal. Canned beans are a good substitute for dried beans which require a long cooking time. Mexican Hot Pot enhances the flavor of canned beans with traditional Mexican seasonings such as onion, garlic, red pepper, oregano and cumin.

Salsa Chicken & Rice Skillet

# Salsa Chicken & Rice Skillet

**1 (6.9-ounce) package RICE-A-RONI® Chicken Flavor**
**2 tablespoons margarine or butter**
**1 pound boneless, skinless chicken breasts, cut into**
**    1-inch pieces**
**1 cup salsa**
**1 cup frozen or canned corn, drained**
**1 cup (4 ounces) shredded Cheddar cheese**
**1 medium tomato, chopped (optional)**

[ 1 ] In large skillet over medium heat, sauté rice-vermicelli mix with margarine until vermicelli is golden brown.

[ 2 ] Slowly stir in 2 cups water, chicken, salsa and Special Seasonings. Bring to a boil. Reduce heat to low. Cover; simmer 15 minutes.

[ 3 ] Stir in corn. Cover; simmer 5 minutes or until rice is tender and chicken is no longer pink inside. Top with cheese and tomato, if desired. Cover; let stand 5 minutes for cheese to melt.

*Makes 4 servings*

[ **Notas** ] Salsa can be served as a condiment but also is an excellent flavoring ingredient in recipes. There is no one definition of salsa. It can be so hot that it will sear the roof of your mouth or so mild that you can use it as a dipping sauce. Its ingredients vary depending on the region in which it is made and on the use for which it is intended. It does, however, always contain tomatoes and chiles in some form or another. There are many types of salsa: salsa cruda (chopped fresh tomatoes), salsa fresca (freshly made salsa), salsa verde (a green salsa made with tomatillos) and many speciality salsas made with different types of fruits and chiles.

Zesty Steak Fajita

# Zesty Steak Fajitas

**¾ cup *French's*® Worcestershire Sauce, divided**
**1 pound boneless top round, sirloin or flank steak**
**3 tablespoons taco seasoning mix**
**2 red or green bell peppers, cut into quarters**
**1 to 2 large onions, cut into thick slices**
**¾ cup chili sauce**
**8 (8-inch) flour or corn tortillas, heated**
**Sour cream and shredded cheese (optional)**

[ 1 ] Pour ½ cup Worcestershire over steak in deep dish. Cover and refrigerate 30 minutes or up to 3 hours. Drain meat and rub both sides with seasoning mix. Discard marinade.

[ 2 ] Grill meat and vegetables over medium-hot coals 10 to 15 minutes until meat is medium rare and vegetables are charred, but tender.

[ 3 ] Thinly slice meat and vegetables. Place in large bowl. Add chili sauce and ¼ cup Worcestershire. Toss to coat. Serve in tortillas and garnish with sour cream and cheese.           *Makes 4 servings*

[ **Notas** ] Tortillas can be warmed several ways. The best way to warm tortillas is to sprinkle with a little bit of water, especially if they are dry. Then heat individually in a warm dry skillet, about 30 seconds per side. Stack and cover with a warm tea towel. Wrap the bundle in foil and place in a 200°F oven.

# Salads, Soups & Sides

## Mexican Slaw

1 (6-inch) corn tortilla, cut into thin strips
  Nonstick cooking spray
¼ teaspoon chili powder
3 cups shredded green cabbage
1 cup shredded red cabbage
½ cup shredded carrots
½ cup sliced radishes
½ cup corn kernels
¼ cup coarsely chopped fresh cilantro
¼ cup mayonnaise
1 tablespoon lime juice
2 teaspoons cider vinegar
1 teaspoon honey
½ teaspoon ground cumin
¼ teaspoon salt
¼ teaspoon black pepper

[ 1 ] Preheat oven to 350°F. Arrange tortilla strips in even layer on nonstick baking sheet. Spray strips with cooking spray and sprinkle with chili powder. Bake 6 to 8 minutes or until strips are crisp.

[ 2 ] Combine cabbage, carrots, radishes, corn and cilantro in large bowl. Combine mayonnaise, lime juice, vinegar, honey, cumin, salt and pepper in small bowl. Add mayonnaise mixture to cabbage mixture; toss gently to coat. Top with baked tortilla strips.

*Makes 8 servings*

Beef & Salsa Salad Supreme

# Beef & Salsa Salad Supreme

**1 boneless beef top sirloin steak (about 1 pound)**
**2 teaspoons Mexican seasoning blend or chili powder**
**1 package (8 ounces) assorted torn salad greens**
**1 cup rinsed and drained canned black beans**
**1 cup frozen corn, thawed**
**¼ cup salsa or picante sauce**
**¼ cup red wine vinegar and oil salad dressing**
**1 medium tomato, chopped**

[ 1 ] Heat large nonstick skillet over medium heat. Rub both sides of steak with seasoning. Cook steak in skillet 5 minutes per side to medium-rare or until desired doneness. Transfer steak to cutting board; tent with foil. Let stand 5 minutes.

[ 2 ] Meanwhile, combine salad greens, beans and corn in large bowl. Combine salsa and dressing in small bowl; pour over greens mixture. Toss lightly to coat. Evenly divide on salad plates.

[ 3 ] Carve steak crosswise into ¼-inch-thick strips; evenly divide over salad greens. Sprinkle with tomato. *Makes 4 servings*

# Outrageous Mexican Chicken Salad

**6 cups shredded lettuce**
**1 bag (9 ounces) tortilla chips, crushed (about 3 cups)**
**2 cups cubed cooked chicken**
**1 can (15½ ounces) kidney beans, rinsed and drained**
**1½ cups HIDDEN VALLEY® The Original Ranch® Salad Dressing**
**½ cup (2 ounces) shredded Cheddar cheese**
**Tomatoes and olives**

Combine lettuce, tortilla chips, chicken, beans, dressing and cheese in a large bowl. Garnish with tomatoes and olives.

*Makes 4 to 6 servings*

**Crunchy Layered Beef & Bean Salad**

# Crunchy Layered Beef & Bean Salad

- 1 pound ground beef or turkey
- 2 cans (15 to 19 ounces each) black beans or pinto beans, rinsed and drained
- 1 can (14½ ounces) stewed tomatoes, undrained
- 1⅓ cups *French's®* French Fried Onions, divided
- 1 tablespoon *Frank's® RedHot®* Original Cayenne Pepper Sauce
- 1 package (1¼ ounces) taco seasoning mix
- 6 cups shredded lettuce
- 1 cup (4 ounces) shredded Cheddar or Monterey Jack cheese

[ 1 ] Cook beef in large nonstick skillet over medium heat until thoroughly browned; drain well. Stir in beans, tomatoes, ⅔ cup French Fried Onions, **Frank's RedHot** Sauce and taco seasoning. Heat to boiling. Cook over medium heat 5 minutes, stirring occasionally.

[ 2 ] Spoon beef mixture over lettuce on serving platter. Top with cheese.

[ 3 ] Microwave remaining ⅔ *cup* onions 1 minute on HIGH. Sprinkle over salad. *Makes 6 servings*

# Green Chile Rice

- 1 cup uncooked white rice
- 1 can (about 14 ounces) chicken broth plus water to measure 2 cups
- 1 can (4 ounces) diced mild green chiles
- ½ medium yellow onion, peeled and diced
- 1 teaspoon dried oregano
- ½ teaspoon salt
- ½ teaspoon cumin seeds
- 3 green onions, thinly sliced
- ⅓ to ½ cup fresh cilantro

[ 1 ] Combine rice, broth, chiles, yellow onion, oregano, salt and cumin in large saucepan. Bring to a boil, uncovered, over high heat. Reduce heat to low; cover and simmer 18 minutes or until liquid is absorbed and rice is tender.

[ 2 ] Stir in green onions and cilantro. *Makes 6 servings*

Chicken Tortilla Soup

# Chicken Tortilla Soup

**1 teaspoon oil**
**1 clove garlic, minced**
**1 jar (16 ounces) mild chunky-style salsa**
**1 can (14½ ounces) chicken broth**
**¾ cup water**
**2 tablespoons *Frank's® RedHot®* Original Cayenne Pepper Sauce**
**1 package (10 ounces) fully cooked carved chicken breasts**
**1 can (8¾ ounces) whole kernel corn, undrained**
**1 tablespoon chopped fresh cilantro (optional)**
**1 cup crushed tortilla chips**
**½ cup (2 ounces) shredded Monterey Jack cheese**

[ 1 ] Heat oil in large saucepan over medium-high heat. Cook garlic 1 minute or until tender. Add salsa, broth, water and *Frank's RedHot* Sauce. Stir in chicken, corn and cilantro. Heat to boiling. Reduce heat to medium-low. Cook, covered, 5 minutes.

[ 2 ] Stir in tortilla chips and cheese. Serve hot.

*Makes 4 servings*

# Nacho Cheese Soup

**1 package (about 5 ounces) dry au gratin potatoes**
**1 can (about 15 ounces) whole kernel corn, undrained**
**2 cups water**
**1 cup salsa**
**2 cups milk**
**1½ cups (6 ounces) SARGENTO® Taco Blend Shredded Cheese**
**1 can (about 2 ounces) sliced ripe olives, drained**
**Tortilla chips (optional)**

In large saucepan, combine potatoes, dry au gratin sauce mix, corn with liquid, water and salsa. Heat to a boil; reduce heat. Cover and simmer 25 minutes or until potatoes are tender, stirring occasionally. Add milk, cheese and olives. Cook until cheese is melted and soup is heated through, stirring occasionally. Garnish with tortilla chips.

*Makes 6 servings*

# Grilled Chicken Taco Salad

**1 can (14½ ounces) DEL MONTE® Diced Tomatoes
    with Garlic & Onion**
**⅓ cup thick and chunky salsa, hot or medium**
**2 tablespoons vegetable oil**
**2 tablespoons red wine vinegar or cider vinegar**
**1 large head romaine lettuce, chopped (10 to 12 cups)**
**4 boneless, skinless chicken breast halves, grilled
    and cut into bite-size pieces***
**1 can (8 ounces) kidney beans, drained (optional)**
**1 cup (4 ounces) shredded sharp Cheddar cheese**
**3 cups broken tortilla chips**

*Or, substitute 3 cups cubed cooked chicken.*

[ 1 ] Drain tomatoes, reserving 1 tablespoon liquid. Chop tomatoes; set aside.

[ 2 ] Make dressing in small bowl by blending reserved tomato liquid, salsa, oil and vinegar.

[ 3 ] Toss lettuce with tomatoes, chicken, beans and cheese in large bowl. Add dressing as desired. Add chips; toss. Season with salt and pepper, if desired. Serve immediately.          *Makes 4 servings*

**Tip:** To add variety to the salad, add chopped avocado, sliced green onions, olives, corn, sliced radishes and chopped cilantro, as desired.

# Mexican Fritters

**1 cup water**
**½ cup (1 stick) butter**
**⅓ cup plus 1 teaspoon sugar, divided**
**¼ teaspoon salt**
**¼ teaspoon ground nutmeg**
**1 cup all-purpose flour**
**4 eggs**
**½ teaspoon vanilla**
**Vegetable oil**

[ 1 ] Combine water, butter, 1 teaspoon sugar, salt and nutmeg in 2-quart saucepan. Heat over medium-high heat until butter is melted, stirring occasionally. Increase heat to high. Bring to a full rolling boil.

[ 2 ] Add flour all at once to saucepan; remove from heat. Beat with wooden spoon until mixture forms smooth thick paste. Cook and stir over medium-high heat 1 to 2 minutes until mixture pulls away from side of pan and forms a ball and a film forms on bottom of pan.

[ 3 ] Add eggs, 1 at a time, beating vigorously after each addition until dough is smooth and shiny. Stir in vanilla. Let dough stand at room temperature 15 minutes.

[ 4 ] Heat 1 inch oil in deep, heavy large skillet over medium-high heat to 375°F; adjust heat to maintain temperature. Line baking sheet with paper towels.

[ 5 ] Spoon dough into pastry bag or cookie press fitted with large star tip (about ½ inch). Carefully press dough directly into hot oil in 6-inch-long strips, cutting strips with scissors to detach. Fry strips, 3 or 4 at a time, 5 to 7 minutes until brown, turning once. Gently remove with tongs or slotted spoon; drain well on paper towels. Repeat until all dough has been fried.

[ 6 ] Roll warm strips in remaining ⅓ cup sugar to coat lightly.

*Makes about 18 fritters*

# Tex-Mex Chicken & Rice Chili

**1 package (6.8 ounces) RICE-A-RONI® Spanish Rice**
**2¾ cups water**
**2 cups chopped cooked chicken or turkey**
**1 can (15 or 16 ounces) kidney beans or pinto beans, rinsed and drained**
**1 can (14½ ounces) tomatoes or stewed tomatoes, undrained**
**1 medium green bell pepper, cut into ½-inch pieces**
**1½ teaspoons chili powder**
**1 teaspoon ground cumin**
**½ cup (2 ounces) shredded Cheddar or Monterey Jack cheese (optional)**
**Sour cream and chopped cilantro (optional)**

[ 1 ] In 3-quart saucepan, combine rice-vermicelli mix, Special Seasonings, water, chicken, beans, tomatoes, green pepper, chili powder and cumin. Bring to a boil over high heat.

[ 2 ] Reduce heat to low; simmer, uncovered, about 20 minutes or until rice is tender, stirring occasionally.

[ 3 ] Top with cheese, sour cream and cilantro.

*Makes 4 servings*

**Black Bean Mexicali Salad**

# Black Bean Mexicali Salad

1 can (15 ounces) black beans, rinsed and drained
1 cup fresh or thawed frozen corn
6 ounces roasted red bell peppers, cut into thin strips
   or coarsely chopped
½ cup chopped red or yellow onion, divided
⅓ cup mild chipotle or regular salsa
2 tablespoons cider vinegar
2 ounces mozzarella cheese, cut into ¼-inch cubes

[ 1 ] Place all ingredients except cheese and 1 tablespoon onion in medium bowl. Toss gently to blend well. Let stand 15 minutes to blend flavors.

[ 2 ] Just before serving, gently fold in all but 2 tablespoons cheese. Sprinkle remaining cheese and reserved tablespoon onion on top. Serve immediately.          *Makes 4 to 6 servings*

# Mexican Rice

2 tablespoons butter or margarine
1 cup long-grain white rice*
½ cup chopped onion
2 cloves garlic, finely chopped
1 jar (16 ounces) ORTEGA® Salsa-Thick & Chunky
1¼ cups water*
¾ cup (1 large) peeled, shredded carrot
½ cup frozen peas, thawed (optional)

*For a quick-cook Mexican Rice, use 4 cups instant rice instead of 1 cup long-grain white rice, and 2½ cups water instead of 1¼ cups water. After salsa mixture comes to a boil, cook for a length of time recommended on instant rice package.*

**MELT** butter in large saucepan over medium heat. Add rice, onion and garlic; cook, stirring occasionally, for 3 to 4 minutes or until rice is golden. Stir in salsa, water, carrot and peas. Bring to a boil. Reduce heat to low; cook, covered, for 25 to 30 minutes or until liquid is absorbed and rice is tender.          *Makes 8 servings*

**South-of-the-Border Corn and Onion Soup**

# South-of-the-Border Corn and Onion Soup

**2 cans (13¾ ounces each) chicken broth**
**1 package (16 ounces) frozen whole kernel corn**
**1 cup mild taco sauce**
**1⅓ cups *French's*® French Fried Onions, divided**
**1 tablespoon *Frank's*® *RedHot*® Original Cayenne Pepper Sauce**
**½ teaspoon ground cumin**
**1 cup (4 ounces) shredded Cheddar or Monterey Jack cheese with jalapeño pepper**
**1 can (4 ounces) chopped green chilies, drained**
**1 cup low-fat sour cream**

[ 1 ] Combine chicken broth, corn, taco sauce, ⅔ cup French Fried Onions, **Frank's RedHot** Sauce and cumin in large saucepan. Bring to a boil over high heat, stirring often. Reduce heat to low. Simmer, uncovered, 10 minutes, stirring occasionally.

[ 2 ] Pour one third of the soup into blender or food processor. Cover tightly; blend until puréed. Transfer to large bowl. Repeat with remaining soup, blending in batches. Return all puréed mixture to saucepan.

[ 3 ] Add cheese; whisk until cheese melts and mixture is well blended. Stir in green chilies and sour cream. Cook over low heat until heated through. Do not boil. Ladle soup into individual bowls. Garnish with additional sour cream, if desired. Sprinkle with remaining ⅔ cup onions.

*Makes 6 to 8 servings*

[ **Notas** ] Creamed soups or sopas are commonly served in Mexico as first courses. Serve this delicious soup either as a starter or a lunch entrée. Mexican soups are often served with a wedge of lime which is squeezed into the soup just before eating to freshen the flavor.

Confetti Black Beans

# Confetti Black Beans

1 cup dried black beans
3 cups water
1 can (about 14 ounces) chicken broth
1 bay leaf
1½ teaspoons olive oil
1 medium onion, chopped
¼ cup chopped red bell pepper
¼ cup chopped yellow bell pepper
2 cloves garlic, minced
1 jalapeño pepper,* finely chopped
1 large tomato, seeded and chopped
½ teaspoon salt
⅛ teaspoon black pepper
Hot pepper sauce (optional)

*Jalapeño peppers can sting and irritate the skin, so wear rubber gloves when handling peppers and do not touch your eyes.*

[ 1 ] Sort and rinse black beans. Cover with water; soak overnight. Drain beans. Place in large saucepan. Add chicken broth; bring to a boil over high heat. Add bay leaf. Reduce heat to low; cover and simmer about 1½ hours or until beans are tender.

[ 2 ] Heat oil in large skillet over medium heat. Add onion, bell peppers, garlic and jalapeño pepper; cook 8 to 10 minutes or until onion is tender, stirring frequently. Add tomato, salt and black pepper; cook 5 minutes.

[ 3 ] Add onion mixture to beans; cook 15 to 20 minutes. Remove bay leaf before serving. Serve with hot sauce.        *Makes 6 servings*

Mexican Taco Salad

# Mexican Taco Salad

1 pound ground beef or turkey
1 cup chopped onion
1 cup **ORTEGA**® **Salsa-Thick & Chunky**
¾ cup water
1 package (1¼ ounces) ORTEGA Taco Seasoning Mix
1 can (15 ounces) kidney or pinto beans, rinsed and
    drained
1 can (4 ounces) ORTEGA Diced Green Chiles
6 tortilla shells *or* 3 cups tortilla chips
6 cups shredded lettuce, *divided*
¾ cup (3 ounces) shredded Nacho & Taco blend cheese,
    *divided*

SUGGESTED TOPPINGS

   Sour cream, guacamole, ORTEGA Thick & Smooth
   Taco Sauce

**COOK** beef and onion until beef is brown; drain. Stir in salsa, water
and seasoning mix. Bring to a boil. Reduce heat to low; cook for 2 to
3 minutes. Stir in beans and chiles.

**LAYER** ingredients as follows in *each* shell: *1 cup* lettuce, *¾ cup*
meat mixture, *2 tablespoons* cheese and desired toppings.

*Makes 6 servings*

## [ Notas ] Toppings add variety and perk up the flavor of this and
other salads. Try sliced radishes, chopped cilantro, diced avocado and
diced tomatoes for other topping ideas.

# Sweets

## Mexican Brownies

**1 box (19.8 ounces) brownie mix plus ingredients
   to prepare brownies**
**2 teaspoons cinnamon**
**1 package (8 ounces) cream cheese, softened**
**½ cup dulce de leche (See Notas)**
**2 tablespoons powdered sugar**

[ 1 ] Prepare and bake brownies according to package directions, adding cinnamon to batter. Cool completely.

[ 2 ] Beat cream cheese in medium bowl with electric mixer at medium speed until smooth. Add dulce de leche and powdered sugar; beat until well blended and creamy. Frost brownies. Serve immediately. For a richer flavor, refrigerate 8 hours or overnight.

*Makes 16 brownies*

[ **Notas** ] Dulce de leche is caramelized condensed milk widely used in Mexican desserts. It is sold in cans in most large supermarkets. Or, make dulce de leche by heating 1 cup whole milk and ½ cup granulated sugar just to a boil; reduce heat to medium-low and cook 30 minutes or until caramel in color, stirring occasionally. Remove from heat and cool completely. Stir in ¼ teaspoon vanilla. If using homemade dulce de leche, omit 2 tablespoons powdered sugar in the recipe.

Mexican Wedding Cookies

# Mexican Wedding Cookies

**1 cup pecan pieces or halves**
**1 cup (2 sticks) butter, softened**
**2 cups powdered sugar, divided**
**2 cups all-purpose flour, divided**
**2 teaspoons vanilla**
**⅛ teaspoon salt**

[ 1 ] Place pecans in food processor. Process using on/off pulsing action until pecans are ground but not pasty.

[ 2 ] Beat butter and ½ cup powdered sugar in large bowl with electric mixer at medium speed until light and fluffy. Gradually add 1 cup flour, vanilla and salt. Beat at low speed until well blended. Stir in remaining 1 cup flour and ground nuts. Shape dough into ball; wrap in plastic wrap. Refrigerate 1 hour or until firm.

[ 3 ] Preheat oven to 350°F. Shape dough into 1-inch balls. Place 1 inch apart on ungreased cookie sheets.

[ 4 ] Bake 12 to 15 minutes or until golden brown. Let cookies stand on cookie sheets 2 minutes.

[ 5 ] Meanwhile, place 1 cup powdered sugar in 13×9-inch glass dish. Transfer hot cookies to powdered sugar. Roll cookies in powdered sugar, coating well. Let cookies cool in sugar.

[ 6 ] Sift remaining ½ cup powdered sugar over sugar-coated cookies before serving. Store tightly covered at room temperature or freeze up to 1 month.                  *Makes about 4 dozen cookies*

[ **Notas** ] Mexican Wedding Cookies are rich buttery cookies that are traditionally individually wrapped in colored tissue paper. Serve with a cup of Mexican coffee or hot chocolate for a special morning or afternoon treat.

**Caramel Flan**

# Caramel Flan

**1 cup sugar, divided**
**2 cups half-and-half**
**1 cup milk**
**1½ teaspoons vanilla**
**6 eggs**
**2 egg yolks**
**Hot water**
**Fresh strawberries**

[ 1 ] Preheat oven to 325°F. Heat 5½- to 6-cup ring mold in oven 10 minutes or until hot.

[ 2 ] Heat ½ cup sugar in heavy medium skillet over medium-high heat 5 to 8 minutes or until sugar is completely melted and deep amber color, stirring frequently. *Do not allow sugar to burn.*

[ 3 ] Immediately pour caramelized sugar into ring mold. Holding mold with potholder, quickly rotate to coat bottom and sides evenly with sugar. Place mold on wire rack. *Caution: Caramelized sugar is very hot; do not touch it.*

[ 4 ] Combine half-and-half and milk in heavy 2-quart saucepan. Heat over medium heat until almost simmering; remove from heat. Add remaining ½ cup sugar and vanilla; stir until sugar is dissolved.

[ 5 ] Lightly beat eggs and egg yolks in large bowl until blended but not foamy; gradually stir in milk mixture. Pour custard into ring mold.

[ 6 ] Place mold in large baking pan; pour hot water into baking pan to depth of ½ inch. Bake 35 to 40 minutes or until knife inserted into center of custard comes out clean.

[ 7 ] Remove mold from water bath; place on wire rack. Let stand 30 minutes. Cover and refrigerate 1½ to 2 hours or until thoroughly chilled.

[ 8 ] To serve, loosen inner and outer edges of flan with tip of small knife. Cover mold with rimmed serving plate; invert and lift off mold. Garnish with strawberries. Spoon melted caramel over each serving.

*Makes 6 to 8 servings*

Mexican Coffee with Chocolate and Cinnamon

# Mexican Coffee
# with Chocolate and Cinnamon

**6 cups water**
**½ cup ground dark roast coffee**
**2 cinnamon sticks**
**1 cup half-and-half**
**⅓ cup chocolate syrup**
**¼ cup packed dark brown sugar**
**1 teaspoon vanilla**
**1 cup whipping cream**
**¼ cup powdered sugar**
**½ teaspoon vanilla**
**Ground cinnamon**

[ 1 ] Place water in coffee maker. Add coffee and cinnamon sticks to coffee filter. Combine half-and-half, chocolate syrup, brown sugar and vanilla in coffee pot. Place coffee pot with cream mixture in coffee maker. Brew coffee; coffee will drip into coffee pot with cream mixture.

[ 2 ] Meanwhile, place whipping cream in cold deep bowl. Add sugar and vanilla; beat with electric mixer at high speed until stiff peaks form. Pour coffee into individual coffee cups; top with dollop of whipped cream. Sprinkle with ground cinnamon.

*Makes 10 to 12 servings*

[ **Notas** ] Mexican cinnamon is also known as canela. Cinnamon is used to flavor both savory and sweet Mexican dishes. The cinnamon sticks used in Mexican cooking are papery thin with rougher edges and are less expensive than the traditional variety found in supermarkets. If the cinnamon sticks aren't added to the coffee filter, they can be used as stirrers for coffee and hot chocolate. The flavor of the cinnamon seeps into the beverages while you are stirring.

Rice Pudding Mexicana

# Rice Pudding Mexicana

**1 package (4-serving size) rice pudding**
**1 tablespoon vanilla**
**¼ teaspoon ground cinnamon**
  **Dash ground cloves**
**¼ cup sliced almonds**
  **Additional ground cinnamon**

[ 1 ] Prepare rice pudding according to package directions.

[ 2 ] Remove pudding from heat; stir in vanilla, ¼ teaspoon cinnamon and cloves. Divide evenly among 6 individual dessert dishes.

[ 3 ] Top with almonds and additional cinnamon. Serve warm.

*Makes 6 servings*

# Mexican Ice Cream Pie

**1 cup butter pecan ice cream, softened**
**1 prepared (9-inch) chocolate crumb pie crust**
**¾ cup caramel ice cream topping**
**2 cups coffee ice cream, softened**
**1 jar (12 ounces) hot fudge topping**
**½ cup coffee-flavored liqueur (optional)**

[ 1 ] Spread butter pecan ice cream in bottom of pie crust. Freeze 20 minutes or until semi-firm.

[ 2 ] Spread caramel topping over butter pecan ice cream. Freeze 20 minutes or until caramel is firm.

[ 3 ] Spread coffee ice cream over caramel. Freeze pie until firm, 6 hours or overnight.

[ 4 ] Combine hot fudge topping and coffee-flavored liqueur, if desired, in small saucepan over medium heat; stir until well blended and hot.

[ 5 ] Allow pie to stand at room temperature 15 minutes before serving. Drizzle with hot fudge topping mixture.

*Makes 6 to 8 servings*

Spanish Churros

# Spanish Churros

**1 cup water**
**¼ cup (½ stick) butter**
**6 tablespoons sugar, divided**
**¼ teaspoon salt**
**1 cup all-purpose flour**
**2 eggs**
**Vegetable oil for frying**
**1 teaspoon ground cinnamon**

[ 1 ] Place water, butter, 2 tablespoons sugar and salt in medium saucepan; bring to a boil over high heat. Remove from heat; add flour. Beat with spoon until dough forms ball and releases from side of pan. Vigorously beat in eggs, 1 at a time, until mixture is smooth. Spoon dough into pastry bag fitted with large star tip. Pipe 3×1-inch strips onto waxed-paper-lined baking sheet. Freeze 20 minutes.

[ 2 ] Pour vegetable oil into 10-inch skillet to ¾-inch depth. Heat oil to 375°F. Transfer frozen dough to hot oil with large spatula. Fry 4 or 5 churros at a time until deep golden brown, 3 to 4 minutes, turning once. Remove churros with slotted spoon to paper towels; drain.

[ 3 ] Combine remaining 4 tablespoons sugar and cinnamon. Place in paper bag. Add warm churros, 1 at a time; close bag and shake until churros is coated with sugar mixture. Remove to wire rack. Repeat with remaining sugar mixture and churros; cool completely. Store tightly covered at room temperature or freeze up to 3 months.

*Makes about 3 dozen cookies*

# [ Notas ]
The next time you are hungry for a donut, try churros instead. Churros are Mexican pastries made of fried dough sprinkled with cinnamon sugar. For an authentic Mexican treat, heat some thick chocolate sauce for dipping.

Cajeta y Frutas

# Cajeta y Frutas

**1 (14-ounce) can sweetened condensed milk**
**3 cups whipped topping**
**Sliced strawberries or peaches, or fresh berries**
**Fresh mint leaves**

[ 1 ] Simmer milk in top of covered double boiler over medium-low heat 1 to 2 hours or until milk is light caramel colored, stirring occasionally.

[ 2 ] Pour cooked milk into a mixer bowl with paddle attachment. Beat on low speed until milk is smooth and creamy Bring milk to room temperature. Fold in whipped topping; stir just until smooth. Transfer to bowl. Cover; refrigerate 2 hours or overnight. Divide among small dishes. Serve with fruit; garnish with mint.          *Makes 12 servings*

# Mexican Coffee

**6 cups hot brewed coffee**
**1 (14-ounce) can EAGLE BRAND® Sweetened Condensed Milk (NOT evaporated milk)**
**½ cup coffee liqueur**
**2 teaspoons vanilla extract**
**⅓ cup tequila (optional)**
**Ground cinnamon (optional)**

[ 1 ] In medium saucepan over medium heat, combine coffee, EAGLE BRAND® and liqueur. Heat through, stirring constantly. Remove from heat; stir in vanilla and tequila (optional).

[ 2 ] Sprinkle each serving with cinnamon. Store leftovers covered in refrigerator.          *Makes 8 cups coffee*

## Acknowledgments

The publisher would like to thank the companies and organizations listed below for the use of their recipes and photographs in this publication.

Birds Eye Foods

Del Monte Corporation

Dole Food Company, Inc.

EAGLE BRAND®

The Golden Grain Company®

The Hidden Valley® Food Products Company

Jennie-O Turkey Store®

MASTERFOODS USA

National Pork Board

Ortega®, A Division of B&G Foods, Inc.

Reckitt Benckiser Inc.

Sargento® Foods Inc.

Unilever

Walnut Marketing Board

# Index

# Index